Dr. Landin's
89 ESSENTIAL TIPS
for New College Students

J.M. Landin, PhD

Copyright © 2016 J.M. Landin

All rights reserved.

ISBN: 1523664215
ISBN-13: 978-1523664214

For McKay and Sumer

INTRODUCTION

For every ten college freshmen you meet on the first day of Fall Semester, only four will persevere to commencement. Three of the ten will leave school and not come back. The remaining three will transfer to another school or be significantly delayed by the challenges of life.

The most significant factors impacting students' ability to graduate: 1) money, 2) isolation, 3) poor preparation for college-level work, and 4) lack of skills for independent living. This short collection of advice can help with all these issues, as well as others that may arise.

At some point in the next few years, you WILL find yourself in a jam. This little book can help you get out. Even better, it may prevent a few of those messes.

While each of us is 100% unique, our attempts at classes and college living are surprisingly similar. I see many students make the same mistakes I made. If you ask for advice (or read this book), you'll often get answers for average people. It may be good advice, but not all of it may apply to you. Only you know your limitations, capabilities, future goals, family/home situations, financial constraints, etc. Ultimately, you make the decisions for your life. You reap the rewards and the consequences of those decisions. Accepting that responsibility is what it means to grow-up.

Now, if you are anything like I was at 18, you will scan through these pages and think "I know that" or "I won't be in that situation." Then, before the year is over, you'll end up in that very situation. **Keep this book.** I made it small for a reason – it's light and doesn't take up much space in your room. It's even useful after college. So hold on to it.

You can do this.

CONTENTS

The College Experience 1
State of Mind 10
Dealing with Professors, Advisors & College Staff 14
Email 18
Choosing Classes 21
Being Prepared 26
During Class 30
Grades 36
Studying 40
Reading & Projects 47
Taking Tests 52
Making Connections 59
Growing Up 62
Safety 71
Money Money Money 74

Appendices 81

The College Experience

1. Your main focus is...

ACADEMICS, ACADEMICS, ACADEMICS.

Learning is your job in college. Show up to meetings (classes) even if they start at 8 a.m. or if they're boring. Hand in assignments by their deadlines. Don't ask for special treatment if extracurricular activities get in the way of your job.

Sometimes your job is easy and you can get your work done quickly; sometimes you need to put in overtime.

Your professor is your boss: s/he assigns the work, evaluates your performance, and makes the rules. Your advisor is a mentor. Treat each one accordingly.

Even though school's your job and you have responsibilities, it can be a great job! Enjoy your time, make new friends, get involved. Just make sure you always remember why you're there.

2. Got Academics down? Now pay attention to…

Developing Life Skills – Living independently takes practice, and you will make mistakes. College allows you a few years to learn to cook, clean, do laundry, pay bills, etc. [See **Growing Up**]

Networking – In just four years, you'll head out to start your own career. Other students, friends, job supervisors, even some professors can all help you – and you may be able to help them in time. Build a network of interesting, trustworthy, helpful people, and create an atmosphere of support. Give more than you take, and always say thank you. [See **Making Connections**]

Having Fun – Try something new: sports, clubs, Greek life, parties, events. Have a good time. Blow off steam. Make friends.

As long as you've got ACADEMICS covered, enjoy!

3. You WILL Mess Up.

Those first two tips you just read? You'll mess them up. Yes, at some point in the next four years, you will put "having fun" before "academics." You will utterly screw up cooking or paying bills on time. You will fail a class. You will lose your scholarship. You might get yourself into a very dangerous situation.

No book, advisor, mentor, or parent can compete with the best teacher of all – experience.

In my view, we face four types of experiences:

- Positive – Many of us don't pay attention to the lessons we can learn from positive experiences. What did you do right? How can you do that again? Reflect on the positives, and you'll probably also enjoy your life a lot more!
- Uncomfortable – These are the most common negative experiences. You fail a test or class because you didn't study properly, or didn't ask for help early enough, or didn't go to class. You turn all your clothes pink in the laundry. You end up with a huge water bill because you didn't get a leak repaired. These experiences ensure you grow up and start accepting minor discomfort today for an easier tomorrow. No one else will tell you what you can or can't do anymore. That's for you to figure out as an adult.

- Repeated – Are you enduring the same uncomfortable experiences over and over again? You're failing to learn from them. Why? Do you expect someone else to fix the problem? Are you blaming others? Or punishing yourself? Maybe you feel that you can't control yourself? If you find yourself continually in the same situation, you are heading down a slippery slope. Get help from a counselor to break these cycles.
- Hazardous – These experiences are the worst of all: addiction, rape, abuse, untreated mental illness, etc. If you end up in one of these situations, you need help immediately. Contact police, a counselor, professor, advisor... anyone. You cannot fix this yourself.

Research indicates that one of the most important experiences people gain from their college experience is FINISHING. Setting this goal and completing it by overcoming obstacles and persevering even when you think you can't – these are some of the most important lessons you can learn from college.

Do not give up. Keep trying and keep moving forward.

"With freedom comes responsibility."

– Eleanor Roosevelt

4. Learn How to Learn.

If you're anything like me, you did pretty well in high school. So you should do pretty well in college, right?
Wrong!

College is a whole new game. It's not just one step up from high school, it's ten. And if your high school education was anything less than spectacular, you WILL struggle. At some point – maybe your freshman year, maybe your senior year – you will do poorly.

First, **don't panic**.

Second, **don't get angry** at your professor or your advisor. Talk to them – they want you to do well. Actually follow their advice. You are not the first student to have this problem.

Finally, recognize that this problem relates to HOW you study, not whether you're smart enough to be in college. You ARE smart enough and you CAN do this. You just have to adapt (start by reading the **Studying** chapter).

The most common theme running through my students' reflections is: "I did well in high school so I thought I'd do well in college. But I WAY underestimated the work." You're not alone. You will adjust. It will get easier.

5. Join a club and plan to become an officer.

Many students think clubs will look good on a resumé. They do, but only if you're involved and participating. On a resumé, leading one club looks better than just being a member of three. Set yourself apart by developing leadership and organizational skills.

Join a few clubs your first year. Meet the club members, consider your club's educational or service goals. Get involved: go on club trips; volunteer at club activities; organize an event; recommend speakers for your club's meetings; suggest creative ways to serve your college or local community, or to promote the group.

Pick the club you enjoy most, and run for Secretary or Representative during your sophomore or junior year. Then, you can run for Treasurer, Vice President, or President your junior/senior year.

6. Stay at school over (most) weekends.

Immerse yourself in your new world. If you spend too much time at home, seeing your old friends or going to your old hangouts, you're not growing. Part of what you learn at college is how to make new friends, try new activities, explore new places. You can't do that if you're not there.

Many students feel isolated at school – it's one of the most common reasons students drop out. While going home makes you feel better temporarily, it may make the problem worse (you're not fully invested in your current life). Get a weekend job or volunteer. Join a club and arrange a weekend activity. Coordinate a study group that meets on weekends. Yell "Anyone want to order pizza?" down your hall. Remember that this isolation is normal – and temporary.

7. Study abroad.

Go somewhere. Soak in a new culture. Immerse yourself in a different language. Appreciate how many similarities we have. Eat new foods, explore regional history, and live like a local.

If you can't afford an entire semester away, share your skills on a service Spring Break. Odds are, you won't get another chance like this until you retire.

Plan one of these experiences for your junior year.

8. What if you don't like it here?

Give yourself a year, but if you really don't feel comfortable at your college, consider transferring or taking a break for a year.

Reflect on your goals – they need to match your college.

The two main ways schools differ are in class size and available resources. At large research universities, you'll have larger classes (especially freshman and sophomore years), but you'll have a wider range of courses and majors, as well as access to top-notch researchers (for internships or jobs), excellent library resources, and special events. At smaller colleges, you'll get to know your professors and peers better; class sizes are smaller, but you'll need to work a little harder to find cutting-edge opportunities.

Also, each college or university specializes in focus areas. Land-grant universities often concentrate on practical pursuits such as agriculture or engineering. Some schools have professional programs (e.g., medical schools) that guide their focus. Others are well-regarded for specialty fields like bioethics or international relations.

If you consider leaving, make sure you have a good reason. Head for a better opportunity. Don't just leave to get away.

State of Mind

9. Challenge your beliefs.

In high school, you learned a lot… but it probably wasn't very controversial. In the "real world," of course, there's a boatload of controversy. You WILL start to address some of those issues in college. Listen. Question. Keep an open mind.

One BIG problem many college students face occurs as they develop opinions that differ from their family or community views. This scenario can lead students to feel torn between their new world and their old world. It's a struggle, but give it time. Eventually, you will find a way to resolve it. Respecting and seeing the positive in each set of views is a good way to start.

10. Good Grades ≠ Good Person.

As a professor and advisor, I've met some awesome students. These students weren't awesome because of their grades; some had high GPAs, some struggled in school. I wanted to help them (by writing letters of recommendation, mentoring independent projects, etc.) because they're great people – polite, enthusiastic, responsible, honest, and accepting.

If you act rude, dishonest, critical, or self-centered… well, that's up to you. Just don't expect people to like or help you (even if you have a 4.0 GPA).

11. Don't avoid classes. Get excited by them.

You're paying a lot of money for these classes. Go.*

Not interested? Figure out how they relate to something you ARE interested in. Example: Let's say you have to take a biology class but you hate biology. If you like soccer, biology involves anatomy (why you got that broken ankle), genetics (why you're so tall), cellular functions (how food gets converted to energy and movement) and photosynthesis (where all that oxygen you're using comes from).

If you don't like a class, it's probably because you don't really understand it as well as you should. Get a tutor. Talk to your professor about suggested learning techniques. Go online to find videos explaining neat aspects of the topic.

The point is… if you're avoiding a class, you should probably be putting MORE effort in, not less.

You're paying $300-3,000 PER CLASS (tuition and fees depending on public/private, in-state/out-of-state). Considering that those classes meet 30–45 times during the semester, you're paying ~$25 per lecture whether you show up or not. If you bought a $25 ticket to an event or show, you'd go!

12. See in greys (not black & white).

You'll be learning about topics from different points of view. As a result, the world will get much more confusing... but much richer.

13. Catastrophes

Sometimes life throws you a curveball. Some students get cancer or severe illnesses; some have really bad accidents or injuries; some deal with the loss or illness of a relative.

PLEASE acknowledge that these events need to be dealt with first. If you try to take a full load of classes in between radiation treatments or surgeries, your recovery will be slower... or worse.

You CAN take a semester off (or 5 years!) to take care of more important matters.

When you come back, start slowly. Take some easier classes or attend part-time. Relapses can be worse than the original problem.

Dealing with
Professors, Advisors & College Staff

Illustration by J. Knorr

14. Be honest. Be polite.

Faculty, advisors, and staff know you'll make mistakes. They want to help* you. If you're not honest (with them and with yourself), they can't give you the best advice.

If you're asking for help, you may start by looking at what you did wrong. Admit to your error and ask how you can fix it. Always be polite when asking for help (especially if you need someone to do extra work to fix your mess).

If people go out of their way to help you, send a thank you note to them AND to their supervisor.

*"Help" does not always mean "fix" or "solve" the problem. It may be that you deal with the consequences of your decisions. If you got yourself into a difficult situation, you're going to have to work to get yourself out.

15. There are good and bad professors/advisors. Learn to tell which is which.

(HINT: it has nothing to do with grade distributions or how fun they are.)

A great teacher or advisor challenges you ("difficult"), attempts to inspire you ("enthusiastic"), and provides you tools to help yourself (study tips, learning goals, practice problems, homework, assignments, etc.).

If you read a professor's evaluations, realize that most students distinguish only between "easy" and "hard" classes. "Easy" classes are often a waste of time and money (See **Grades**). Read comments carefully to determine which "difficult" professors are enthusiastic and helpful, and which are not.

16. Keep things in perspective.

Professors, advisors, and staff deal with students in real life-and-death situations (severe accidents, cancer, abuse, homelessness, addiction, etc.).

A cold, a flat tire, or an F may seem like a big deal… but it's not.

17. Jump through hoops.

Filling out forms, applying for permissions or awards, resolving errors, and following up with paperwork are aspects most students don't consider as part of their college career. These standard procedures, though, can affect whether you complete a program, delay graduation, or drop out.

No one likes this stuff. If you want a loan, or if you need to drop a class after a deadline, or your advisor forgot to submit a form, YOU will have to follow through.

Ask your advisor or departmental personnel (office assistants are often the most important people you'll meet!) what steps are necessary to reach your desired outcome. Write these steps down! Confirm your list with the person helping you. Ask how long each step should take. Follow through with as many steps as you can at that moment (always walk any physical forms from one office to another if possible). Write the remaining steps in your calendar and follow up with the appropriate department or person each step of the way.

There will be many times in your life when you'll need to jump through hoops (imagine getting a mortgage and buying a house). Practice now.

Email

18. Explain your efforts.

Ask your question; then explain how you tried to find the answer yourself. By doing this, you may find the answer on your own. If not, it will allow folks to better help you by knowing what you've already tried or how you're thinking about the problem.

Hint: if you're emailing a professor about a class administration issue (how grades are calculated, attendance policy, etc.), ALWAYS check the syllabus first.

19. If your email is longer than 2 paragraphs, edit it.

Odds are, the person you're emailing deals with hundreds of student emails. Ask your question, explain how you tried to answer it yourself and where you got stuck. Say "Thank you". Then send.

Longer emails are often long-winded attempts to explain why you deserve special treatment, why a class rule is "unfair," or why it's someone else's fault.

If you really do have an issue that requires more explanation, just request an appointment.

20. Watch your language.

When you're frustrated or angry, it's easy to write something you'll regret later. Read your email aloud while pretending you're standing in front of the recipient.

By the way, your professor should be addressed as "Dr." or "Professor." Avoid "Mr./Mrs." and NEVER use "Hey" or "Yo."

21. Resend

If you haven't heard from your professor or advisor in three business days, 1) check to make sure you haven't violated any of the above, then 2) resend.

22. NEVER. EVER. E V E R ...
email the professor while you're in class.

Choosing Classes

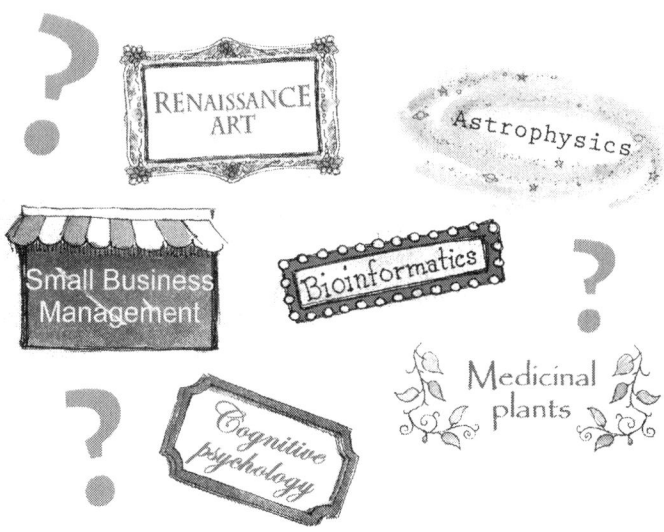

23. Take the professor, not the class.

Have an awesome class? Find out what other courses that professor teaches.

Ask around. Who taught the classes that inspired your friends or made them see the world differently? Look up that professor, and see what classes s/he teaches.

Know of a faculty researcher you're interested in working with? Get to know each other through a class. Then ask about opportunities in their lab.

24. Balance your classes.

In your first two years, balance your course load:
Take mostly moderate-level courses with 1 or 2 difficult and 1 or 2 enjoyable classes. Never take more than 2 "have-to" classes (required ones you dread) in a semester.

Course numbers can guide you: 100-level courses are generally for freshmen, 200-level for sophomores, 300-level for juniors, 400-level for seniors, and 500+ numbers are for graduate courses. As the numbers go up, so should the complexity of the topic.

25. Finding out what you DON'T like can be more important than what you DO like.

It's easier to change your major in college than to change careers 10 years from now. Use jobs, classes, internships, and volunteer activities to test the waters. Many times, you'll realize the subject you thought you liked is not what you imagined. Don't be afraid to shift your focus. Use college as an opportunity to explore.

26. Each semester, take one course JUST because it looks interesting.

You'll enjoy school more... and it might just open your eyes to exciting, unexpected possibilities or career paths.

27. Majoring in Education?
Double major with your subject.

Unfortunately, an education degree has a low rate of return (salaries are generally low). If you're interested enough in a topic to devote to teaching it, why not make it a major? It'll also give you additional employment opportunities in the future.

Majoring in **Art, Social Work, Gender Studies**, etc.? Same advice applies. Consider your future career and add a major to gain skills. For example, if you're an artist, you'll probably need to know about business. And if you're majoring in Art but can't stomach business classes, you may need to reconsider your career goals.

28. Minors (usually) don't impress.

A minor, if it's closely related to your major, often requires just a few extra courses. It's easy. And everyone knows it.

If you're going to get a minor, make it something unusual.
Human Biology major? Minor in philosophy, botany or communication.
English major? Minor in business, geology or history.

Then again, if you're interested enough to get a minor, why not double-major? It shows you don't shy away from a challenge.

29. Enroll ASAP.

As soon as you can register for class, do. The best courses fill up quickly. When you're a freshman, you register last. Make sure you have back-up classes ready.

As you accumulate more credit hours, you'll register earlier. The best thing about honor/scholar or student-athlete programs is that you often register earlier. It's a worthwhile perk.

30. Never waste your time or money on an "Easy A."

You'll spend about 45 hours in class over the semester (plus more time working on assignments or studying). The cost of that class can be hundreds or thousands of dollars. If, at the end of the semester, you leave with an A and no new knowledge, you've wasted a lot of time and money. Grades don't matter anymore [see **Grades**]; learning is everything.

Education is an investment in yourself. A diploma or a certain GPA doesn't mean anything if you have no skills or knowledge. You'll take the skill sets and knowledge with you wherever you roam in the future. No one will be able to take that from you. Value it.

Being Prepared

31. ALWAYS read the syllabus.

The syllabus is like a contract. It should state the expected outcomes for the course (what you should focus on), the professor's rules, class projects, and important dates. Record these dates in your calendar at the start of the semester. Refer back to the syllabus when administrative questions arise.

32. Learn to keep a calendar*.

At the beginning of the semester, record your class meetings, important events, and deadlines for the whole semester. Keep your calendar with you at all times so you can make appointments or look ahead.

It doesn't matter whether your calendar is paper or digital, daily or weekly, home-made or store-bought. Try one… if you're prepared and organized, it works for you. If you miss appointments or test days sneak up on you, try a different type of calendar. You've got at least eight semesters to figure out what works.

Trust me … life will get even busier in the future. So learn to organize your time, appointments, and activities now.

*See **Appendix A** for examples of calendar systems.

33. Devise a Plan B... for everything.

Life rarely goes according to plan. Get in the habit of devising a back-up plan.

- What if your car doesn't start? You hit traffic? Can't find a parking space?
  Leave early enough to overcome these obstacles.
- What if your designated driver leaves without you?
  Carry contact information for a dependable friend or reputable cab company (and bring enough money to get home).
- What if you lose your cell phone?
  Program your phone with your contact information and all security measures.
- What if your alarm doesn't go off?
  Have another alarm programmed (preferably one that does not rely on electricity).
- What if you fail some courses or can't get into the professional school you wanted?
  Consider other majors/careers (you CAN be happy if you take a different path than you'd originally planned). Delay your graduation. Retake a class (with extra effort and tutoring).

You get the idea.

34. To keep in your backpack:

Your calendar, throat lozenges, ear plugs, extra #2 pencils **with** erasers, extra paper, mini-umbrella, and campus map.

You may not use these items a lot, but you'll be glad they're there when you need them.

35. Wear layers.

College classrooms are notorious for their odd temperatures. Dress for it.

36. Visit classrooms before the first day.

Yes, you will look nerdy. But there won't be a lot of people around to see you (and they'll be looking for their classrooms too).
If you DON'T know where your classrooms are on the first day of class, you'll be frazzled and 300 people will watch as you walk in late and try to find a seat. Even worse, you'll miss the first class because you were sitting in the wrong room. (Yes, it happens ALL the time.)

During Class

37. Always go to class. Take notes (on paper)*. Turn off and stow electronics.

Learning consists of three main parts: the first is ***Attention*** (see **Studying** for *Organization* and *Retrieval*). If you're not in class, you can't possibly pay attention to the material covered.

Taking notes (even if your professor puts notes online) will help you stay attuned to what s/he is saying. Don't write every word; do NOT copy slides (unless there's a definition). Focus on the main concepts your professor describes and write those down in your own words.

If you have a question, write it in the margin of your paper. Then ask your professor after class or during office hours.

Laptops and cell phones WILL distract you – turn them OFF and put them in your backpack. Never take notes on a laptop. Checking your email, social networking, or shopping online is too tempting. Got an online class? Treat it like a regular class. Attend class at a set time. Take notes (on paper). Turn off other distracting electronics.

WHY? Studies have shown that students who take notes on a laptop are more likely to record information verbatim. In other words, they don't PROCESS the information. Less *Attention* and no *Organization*.

* See **Appendix B** for Note-taking hints.

38. Be aware of your professor's job OUTSIDE of teaching:

- preparing grant proposals,
- conducting research,
- supervising graduate and undergraduate students,
- advising,
- serving on department and university committees,
- organizing outreach events,
- attending or presenting at professional conferences,
- writing,
- mentoring students or clubs,
- reviewing books or journal articles,
- volunteering his/her expertise for community service,
- filing paperwork and jumping through hoops for his/her own careers and research,
- maintaining records,
- complying with federal and state standards,
- managing funds, etc.

Try to recognize that teaching is only PART of the job – an important and enjoyable part, but professors have many demands on their time. PLEASE read the syllabus before asking class administration questions ("When's the test?", "What documentation do I need for an excused absence?", etc.).

39. Be aware of your professor's role in teaching:

- planning the course and writing the syllabus,
- presenting information (hopefully in a clear yet challenging way),
- producing assignments and assessments,
- grading and giving feedback,
- holding office hours (your chance to ask questions).

S/he does NOT have to individually re-teach material you missed due to an absence*, supply you with notes, entertain you, or offer you extra credit.

*NEVER *ask a professor "Did I miss anything important?" Of course you did!*

40. Don't ask for extra credit.

Extra credit means the instructor has to spend extra time creating and grading an assignment. If a professor is going to offer extra credit, s/he will make it available for every student, not just you.

41. Eliminate "unfair" and "tricky" from your vocabulary.

"Unfair" means unethical or biased. If you mean to say "That test was challenging" or "This question is difficult," then say that.

"Tricky" implies deceitful. Was the test question "deceitful" or was it "specific" and "detailed?" Maybe there was more than one correct answer, and you had to select the BEST one. That's not "tricky," that's life.

Topics you learn about in college should be challenging and detail-oriented. Be ready.

WARNING: when you use "unfair" or "tricky," you're are placing the blame for your performance on your instructor. So your grade is no longer the result of your knowledge.

If you use these words, step back and ask yourself "Do I REALLY understand this information? Could I explain this concept to someone else?"

Take the responsibility. If you do, you can change any grade by changing your behavior. If you don't, you're powerless.

42. Professors LOVE their subject area.

S/he wants to share that excitement with you (if you let them).

When you talk with your professor, try to avoid saying "I hate this subject" – it's not polite.

If you feel that you hate the topic, ask your professor why s/he loves it so much. You might just be inspired.

43. Your professor wants you to do well.

Many students think that professors are out to fail students. Not true. Your professor wants you to learn. Your grade reflects what you learn. For a professor, there would be no greater experience than for every student in class to EARN an A.

(It's also much easier to grade tests and projects if students do a great job!)

Grades

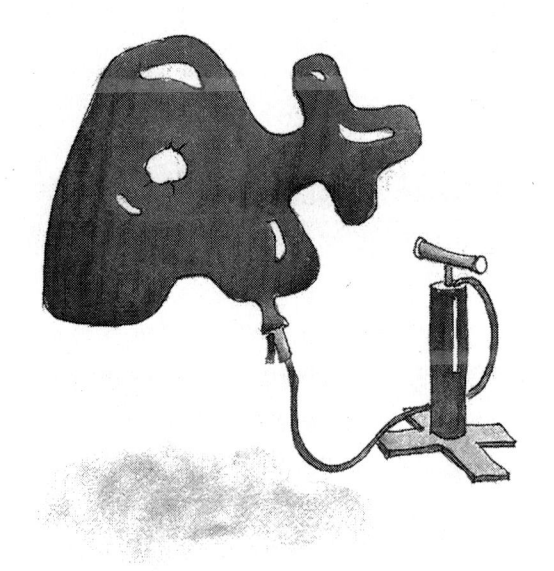

44. Your GPA doesn't matter anymore.

Two reasons:

1. Most students are not going to professional programs or graduate school (which require GPAs) – most future employers will not ask for your GPA;

2. If you ARE going on to a professional program or graduate school, you should really understand the material (and your GPA will reflect that).

45. Grades reflect your understanding.

If you want an A, you'd better know the information backwards and forwards, be able to apply it to any scenario, and explain it at a moment's notice. It is not about memorizing; it's about using information. If you can't do that, you haven't earned an A.

B's and C's are acceptable grades in college. Get used to them.

46. Perfectionist?? Learn to embrace mistakes.

A few students think they need to have perfect grades or projects. In doing so, they often fail to complete the assignments. Finishing and getting an 80% is better than doing stellar work but receiving a D or F for an incomplete or late assignment.

The bigger issue, though, consists of valuing mistakes. Mistakes mean you're trying. Mistakes indicate exploration. Don't stay safe when it comes to knowledge. Ask outlandish questions, investigate wild ideas, discover, and feel free to mess up.

If you don't want to try unless you know you can succeed, well, you won't get very far. Start practicing being "good enough." You are not in college to show off how great you are. You are here to learn and IMPROVE. You can't improve if you're already perfect.

In life, you can't do everything perfectly. You don't have that kind of time. Figure out how to cut some corners (and double-check how your calendar is working [see **Being Prepared**]).

47. Failing.

Failing a class isn't the end of the world (although your parents may make you feel as though it is. Own up to your errors, and remind your folks that you're still trying and making mistakes). You'd better learn from the experience though. If you just failed a difficult class (or a test), get a tutor and try again with a different instructor. Your instructor may have been good, but hearing the same concepts explained in a different way can be helpful.

Put that class in perspective. You have about 50 classes to take before graduation. Failing one or two isn't that big of a deal. But if you quit because you fail, you've missed the point of college (and a big part of growing up).

If you're failing multiple classes in a semester or a year, something bigger is happening. Go visit a counselor – really.

"Our greatest glory is not in never failing, but in rising up every time we fail."
— Ralph Waldo Emerson

Studying

48. It is YOUR responsibility to learn.

A professor, advisor, boss, or parent cannot open your head and pour information inside. You have to WANT to learn and WORK to learn. Challenge yourself. If it's easy or boring, you're not doing it right. Create your own projects (invent a game covering the international impacts of the American Revolution, write a blog post explaining the Law of Supply and Demand, make a sculpture of the human appendicular skeleton) to apply the information. Stop relying on outside influences, like tests and assignments, to force you to learn.

If you're struggling, remember that you were smart enough to get into college. You're smart enough to succeed in college. **Persistence** and **effort** are what count now.

49. Background knowledge weak?

See if there's a Book "for Dummies" on the topic (or even a high school/middle school book). Read it before classes begin. Alternatively, check online for some overview information, videos, or MOOCs (free online courses). You want to develop a general framework of the topic so you can start adding in details.

50. NEVER make flashcards.

They take a ridiculous amount of time to prepare, and have a low success rate. Here's why: you're looking at the information, not creating it. It gives you a false sense that you know the info when you really don't.

Flashcards also isolate information. You're supposed to be connecting concepts, not just memorizing vocabulary words or detached facts. In college, definitions aren't the focus of your classes — relationships and applications are. You can't put that on a flashcard.

What should you do instead? Read on.

51. Studying*: It's not the time, it's the focus.

Most new students "studied" in high school by reading over their notes. This will NOT work anymore. You must start recreating content (*retrieval*) and grading yourself to identify whether you truly know the information or not.

Learning requires *Attention* (addressed in **Classes**), *Organization*, and *Retrieval*. All three aspects involve concentration, persistence, and self-motivation.

Organization: After class, write a small outline or organizational chart (~1/2 page) of the lecture material (Appendix B). Link concepts to each other, and to facts you already know. If there are any topics you don't quite understand, ask your professor, read about them in your textbook, look them up online, find videos, etc. You MUST understand the concept before you can organize it.

Retrieval: Once your outline's ready, turn it over. Use scrap paper or a white board to re-write your outline from memory (no peeking). Repeat until you get it right. Create mnemonics or use the method of loci if you're struggling. Practice re-writing your outline every couple of days (if you're straining to remember, it's working).

Grade yourself. Give yourself one point for each concept you write in the correct location. If you only remember 12 out of 20 items, you earn a 60%. Most students think they know content even when they don't. The grade forces you to face reality.

Have a list of terms or categories to memorize? Fold a paper in half vertically. Write the word/category on one half and the definition or example on the other half. This is your "answer sheet." Make copies of each half, and practice filling in the blank half (switch up the order of your responses).

If you have to identify structures (like anatomy), make and label your own drawings to study (yes, actually draw the structures even if your drawings are terrible). Before the big test, check your knowledge on photographs or unlabeled diagrams.

Apply it:
Now start using the basics you've memorized. Apply the information to scenarios in your life, current events, or your other classes. The more you use the information and make connections, the stronger your memory becomes.

NOTE: *Of my own students who have struggled in class, every one has skipped* Retrieval. *After I suggested this strategy, grades increased an average of 11–26%. This approach is not only more engaging (less boring) than reading over notes, it's actually faster and more effective. Spend 20–30 minutes every few days on* Retrieval *for each class.*

*See **Appendix C** for an *Organization* and *Retrieval* example.

52. Invest in a timer.

Plan a set amount of time to study or work on assignments each day. Setting the timer helps force you to start and you'll concentrate more if you're not constantly looking at the time.

Oftentimes, once you're working on a project, you'll continue even after the buzzer sounds.

53. How much time?

A 3-credit course = 3 hours in class **PLUS 6 hours of active, uninterrupted work outside class** (no checking social media, texting, changing music, etc). If you take 15 credit hours, you should spend ~45 hours per week seriously focused on your classes.

NOTE: *This includes the first two weeks of the semester! Many students feel they have a lot of free time over the first two weeks. These students also feel completely overwhelmed (and regret wasting those first two weeks) by the semester's half-way point. Those first two weeks are the most important time to get organized, plan, check your background knowledge, and start adapting to your schedule (including study time).*

54. SPRING BREAK!!!
(or fall break... or weekends)

A break from class is not a break from studying or assignments. Do rest, do relax. You need downtime. Just realize you are making a decision; as long as you've been putting in your full 45 hours per week, you can take a break. If not, use the time to catch up.

"*Education is what survives when what has been learned has been forgotten.*"

- B.F. Skinner

Reading & Projects

55. To buy or not to buy... the textbook

Textbooks can be expensive (as well as boring and heavy). When the professor doesn't actually use them in the course, well... what a huge waste of money!

On the other hand, the textbooks faculty recommend can be the best books on the market in those fields. You don't have to research and look through dozens of books to find a good one; your professor has already done that for you.

Go to the bookstore and page through each of your texts before classes start. If it looks interesting, buy it. (Sometimes you may even buy a book for a course you're not taking.) If the book doesn't spark your interest, hold off. It will become clear within the first week of class whether you really need to buy the book. You can purchase it then.

If you plan on selling your books back, why not just rent? Or see if the library has a copy.

56. Read paper, not computers.

Print out readings (use double-sided or multiple-page settings to save paper). Circle or arrow important passages, and write questions or summaries in the margins. Interact with the text.

Do NOT rely on underlining or highlighting – those words are the author's, not yours. Write a simple outline or summary of each chapter. Put main ideas in your own words. This method will help you remember the text's information and organization (and if you need to reference it later, you'll know just where to look).

WHY? For now, research indicates that comprehension is stronger when reading paper compared to online.

57. Use audiobooks with classic literature.

Some books are really difficult to read. If you listen to them, and follow along in the book, it's a lot easier to understand complex sentence structure. Take THAT, Geoffrey Chaucer!

58. Break large projects into chunks, and set deadlines for yourself.

Got a big paper due at the end of the semester? Break it down.

Deciding on a topic usually takes longer than you think. Write down a few ideas and mull them over. Anything you can link to your own interests? Or to other classes?

Write an outline using words or phrases (not sentences). If your paper isn't organized, no skill in writing or research will help. Over time, increase detail in your outline. When your outline is 1/3 the length of your paper, put it away for a few days before starting to write. Don't be afraid to re-organize, re-write, or replace your outline.

Using your outline, go ahead and write… and write… and write. Editing will take up the majority of your time AND will whittle down the length of your paper. So don't worry about writing the perfect sentence. Just get it down on paper. THEN examine each paragraph and sentence for clarity.

Editing*:

- Check grammar and spelling.
- Underline nouns and verbs in each sentence. Make sure they match tenses. Try to put them close together.
- **Delete repeated ideas and empty phrases.**
  (In my experience, this is the most common misstep. Stop trying to fill the page! Think about your reader. Are you boring them to tears? Remove duplication and flesh out details instead. Answer the questions How, Why, What If.)
- Replace 'is/are' verbs and the passive voice.
- Make it interesting. Add your personality, experiences and thoughts to create a unique paper.
- Apply information you've learned in class.

Give yourself twice as much time as you think it will take for completing each part of the project. Set your deadline for completion one week before it's actually due. Put your project away for a few days and re-examine it for minor tweaks before submission.

What if your big project is not a paper? You can still use the steps described: Plan, organize, compile, edit, and review.

* See **Appendix D** for editing examples.

Taking Tests

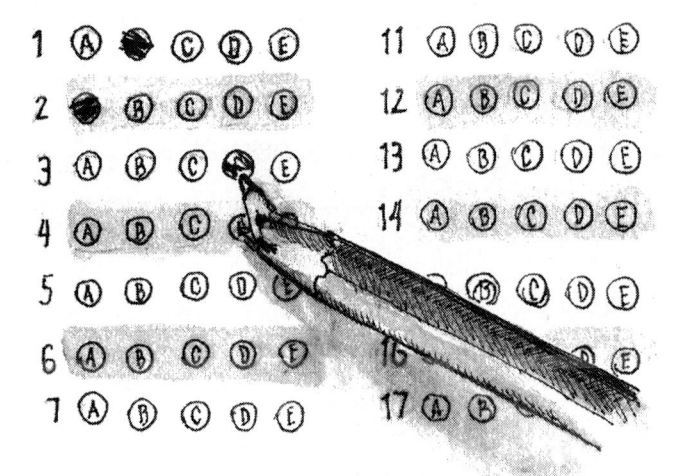

59. Arrive early, arrive prepared.

"Test anxiety" is often the result of poor preparation. Know the material [see **Studying**], get a good night's sleep, eat breakfast, bring a couple pencils WITH erasers... and visit the restroom before the test begins.

Remember, if the test is written well, you will get the grade you deserve.

60. What's the worst that could happen?

You will not be beaten, killed, teased, or harassed by your professor if you earn an F. The very worst thing that could happen is that you have to take the class over again.

You will face big challenges in the future. Tests are **very** minor versions of those challenges. Sometimes your efforts won't be good enough. Sometimes you'll be blindsided. Learn to face these scenarios; do the best you can, accept the results, and adjust your behavior as needed.

61. Too many questions! Too little time!

Expect one to two questions per minute on multiple-choice and fill-in-the-blank tests. The amount of time it takes you to answer reflects how well you know the material.

Think of it this way… how quickly can you answer:
"In what year were you born?" (probably less than 5 seconds)

Now how quickly can you answer:
"In what year did the first lunar landing occur?"

Even if you know the answer, it probably took you a little longer to answer. You had to think a little longer and may not have been sure. You probably waffled a little in your mind before answering.

Basic, straight-forward, fact-based questions need to be answered very quickly. Spend most of your time on the more complex or application-based questions.

62. Don't know the answer? Skip it.

Other questions in the test may "jog your memory." Your test is one giant word bank.

Still don't know? Guess on multiple choice. Never leave a blank. Write what you can for essays (partial credit) BUT BE HONEST. Don't just rewrite the question or make things up. It wastes the grader's time.

63. Underline important words in the question to focus on the main point.

Or, in the case of math word problems, write the important information to the side (x=45, r=0.2, etc). Don't let the specific scenario distract you from the important information.

Remember that your professor may include extraneous information. When you face a problem in real life, you'll have a lot of non-essential information. You need to determine which information is essential to solve the problem.

64. Try answering multiple-choice questions before looking at answer options.

Sometimes all those possible answers make the question more confusing. Treat the question like a "fill-in-the-blank." Jot down the answer you would write, then uncover the possible answers and see if you can find it.

Even if you do poorly on the test, it may help your instructor to see your thought process.

65. Test review offered? Attend!

Seeing what you got wrong on a test is often one of the best ways to learn material. Bring your notes. Highlight any topics you missed. If you can't figure out why your answer was wrong, ask your instructor.

66. Show proper documentation if you want a make-up exam.

Read that syllabus carefully regarding excused absences (these are usually defined by your university). Your instructor cannot just take your word for it that your absence qualifies as excused. You need to provide specific documentation. These rules apply to everyone, including you.

67. Keep your notes for the final exam.

You put a lot of time and effort into your notes over the semester (hopefully). Hang on to them. Mark them up. Highlight topics the instructor brings up multiple times throughout the semester. Write in mnemonics you created. Draw diagrams, organizational schematics, or pictures that help you focus or remember.

68. Keep your notes AFTER the final.

Good class? Have your notes bound by a copy-service provider. You will reference these more than you can imagine (even if the class is not in your major).

69. NEVER EVER CHEAT!

Consequences are high even if you get away with it.

First, if you do get caught, you could be expelled. Try and explain that one to your family and future employers.

Second, you may actually need to know that information in the future (in additional courses or in life). If you do need to know the topic, you'll have to learn it on your own OR screw up when the stakes are higher.

Finally, and most importantly…
you will never forget that you are a cheater.

You should regret taking something you didn't earn.
And it's something you can't go back and fix.

> *"I prefer to be true to myself,
> even at the hazard of incurring the ridicule of others,
> rather than be false, and incur my own abhorrence."*
>
> - Frederick Douglass

Making Connections

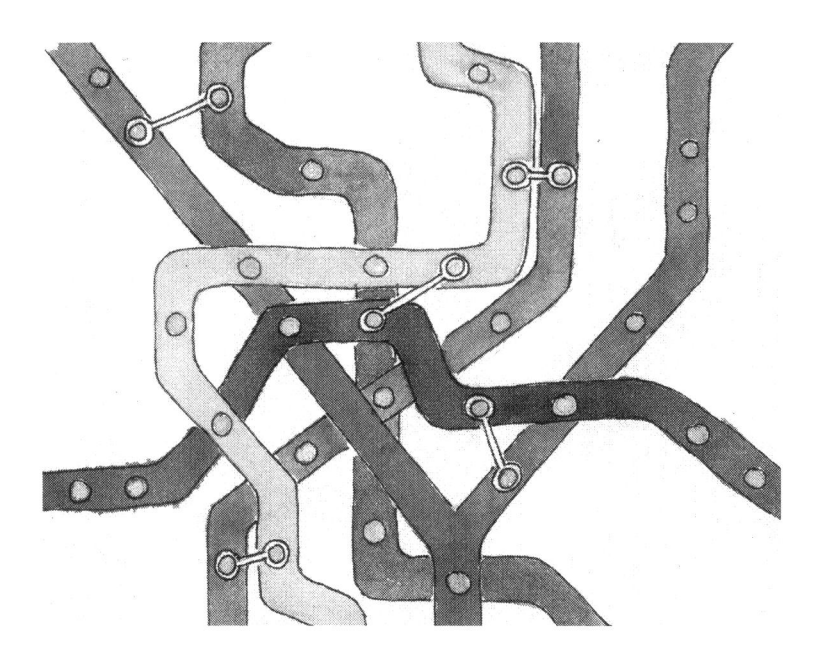

70. Surround yourself with hard-working, responsible, friendly people.

Hard-working, responsible, friendly people won't overwhelm you with requests for help; they complete their share of the project (on time); they make sure you get the credit you deserve. If you're surrounded by people who DON'T do this, politely find a new group of friends.

The people you meet in college can be some of your best connections when you leave college. Show them what a hard-working, responsible, friendly person YOU are. You may just get a job as a result.

What if this awesome person you meet is majoring in business and you're in chemistry – not network material?? Think again. You both could end up at a biotech business. Don't "throw away" good people just because you can't see a direct connection. Keep in touch. You never know what will come up.

71. Develop a good reputation.

Up until now, any terrible decisions you made could be explained by youth and hormones. Now, though, your decisions reflect who you really are. Even at a large university, word will get around.

So be hard-working, responsible and friendly – the kind of person you want to be around. Create symbiotic relationships. If you need a favor, see if there's something you can contribute in return. Match up people with similar interests. If you introduce people, they're likely to introduce you (it's a great way to create future opportunities).

72. Keep records

In the "old days," people used a Rolodex to keep all their business contacts in one place. Today, we have cell phones and social networking sites.

Keep contact information, job title (or major), company, website, notes (like birthday or topics you've discussed, where/when you met), maybe even a photo.

You'll be building a network of business contacts for the next 50 years. Start organizing it now. Your organization of contacts doesn't have to be perfect, but start practicing.

Growing Up

73. Get a job...
in your field (NOT just for money).

Money may be tight now (see **Money, Money, Money**), but the experience you get in college will be worth a LOT more money when you graduate. Start gaining work experience now. Even if it's only 5–10 hours per week, a job will help you build a resumé and see what you like and dislike about the field.

Whatever you do, don't take a job in retail or food service unless that is your intended future career. These jobs are easy to find and, for that reason, do little to set you apart from other graduates when you start on a career path.

Due to the wide range of faculty interests, you may be able to find a unique or adventurous job or internship. Probably at no other point in your life will you be paid to measure how drunk fruit flies get, teach English on a remote tropical island, record octogenarians' memories of Sputnik, or collect data from taste-tests on food additives. These jobs won't make you rich, but WILL give you a great topic of conversation for your future interviews.

*NOTE: If you are working more than 20 hours per week, you are probably not spending enough time on your courses. Consider reducing your work hours OR becoming a part-time student.

74. Ask for help.

I know it seems like asking for help is the opposite of growing up, but understanding your own limitations, seeing how other people tackle problems, appreciating expertise, and acknowledging that others may have a better grasp of the situation are all signs of a remarkably mature person.

In studies of student success, one recurrent theme was *actively seeking help*. Help can come from anywhere – even peers and websites*. Don't ignore a problem. It won't go away.

Most people will want to help you. A lot of questions are pretty easy to answer because many issues deal with terminology or policies specific to the college setting (acronyms, pre-requisites and co-requisites, standing, etc.). If you don't understand or if you're not sure, ask.

While the Internet is a great place to find information, make sure the site is reputable and up-to-date. The best way to do this is to confirm the information with an actual person. Also, your peers will often repeat rumors about university policies, especially those related to grades or graduation. Always confirm what you hear.

75. Take care of yourself*.

In college, there's almost a competition to see who can get by with the least sleep or drink the most coffee. That may be fine to do from time to time, but you need to learn how to sense your body's needs – today and for the long-term.

Set enough time for sleep (at least 8–9 hours... seriously. I cannot emphasize enough the importance of sleep), exercise, healthy meals, daily hygiene, and cleaning your room. Keep up with doctor visits and mental health care. Take a few moments each day to concentrate on how you feel (emotionally and physically).

If you feel you don't have time to take care of yourself, check your calendar organization and approach to studying.

*See **Appendix E** for a basic health checklist.

Many mental health issues arise during the late teens or early twenties. While some stress, anxiety, or depression is normal, get help if these issues feel overwhelming or start impacting your ability to make smart decisions. If a professor, advisor, or friend suggests you seek counseling, go. Often others notice problems before we see them ourselves.
Suicide and alcohol-abuse are the two leading causes of death for college students. Both are preventable.

76. What do you want to do when you grow up?

Many students think they know what career they want after graduation. Most are wrong.

First, you probably don't know about all of the career possibilities out there. How can you choose a career if you don't know it exists?!

Second, you probably haven't experienced much of this career. Being a doctor is more communication and business management than surgery and life-saving. Being a teacher means spending your whole day with people outside your peer-group. Being a designer involves more compromise and less creativity.

Third, you might be aiming for the wrong level.
If you want to be a teacher, have you considered principal? Curriculum developer? Education lobbyist? You've probably met more teachers than curriculum developers.

Never dismiss an awesome career because you don't want to spend a few more years in school.

On the flipside, don't panic if the career you want (e.g., lawyer) slips out of your reach (let's say, because you have a 2.0 GPA and no law school in the country will accept you).

What aspects of that career did you like? List them. Now, using that list, brainstorm other careers that offer those aspects.

You won't graduate and jump into your perfect career. You will probably get a crappy job after college making WAY less money than you expect. Over time, though, jobs turn into a career with a better salary. Just don't expect your parents' lifestyle when you are only 25.

Starting from scratch? Not sure what you want to do?

Get a piece of paper and divide it into three columns. In the first column, list all your interests – all the things you like to do or enjoy. In the second column, write all the activities you're good at – experiences you've had where you excelled. This is no time to be modest. Write down any better than average abilities you have. In the third column, record issues you think are most important to making the world a better place (education, health, creativity, religion, etc.)

Now combine one entry from each column and consider any jobs, internships, classes, or volunteer opportunities that incorporate all three facets.

For example, you may be interested in sports and good at organizing and coordinating activities. You might think educating kids is important. Combine these facets by managing sports camps for underprivileged children.

77. Follow your reality first... then your passion.

Virtually every commencement address tells you to "follow your passion." Ignore them. The people speaking those words are much older than you, and they have been successful in life (or they wouldn't be giving your commencement address).

In reality, Step One is Survival. You can't follow your passion if you don't earn enough money to eat or pay rent. When you can pay for all your necessities, including insurance and a healthy savings account, then you can start thinking about your passion.

For some people, passion isn't that important. They're content just to enjoy life as it comes. Many people, though, search for something more. It may be a social cause, a form of art, or a fantasy dream.

Don't worry if you don't know what your passion is. Sometimes, it finds you. Until then, take time to explore opportunities you didn't know existed or problems you didn't know you could help solve. AND consider the amount of work involved to pursue your goal. You may not have THAT much passion.

Even though "money to survive" comes first, that doesn't mean it's more important. Passion makes a life well-lived.

78. Live Freshman year ON campus.

College is a big transition. Living on campus allows you to make the school your new home and become part of your new community. Don't worry about cooking yet – get the meal plan. Don't worry about setting up utilities, paying rent, or dealing with landlords – it's all covered in your room and board payment. Don't worry about driving – walk everywhere. Sleep more – you're just a few steps from class. Learn about and use the resources offered by your college.

79. Live Senior year OFF campus.

Start making the transition to life away from campus. Learn to cook, set-up and pay utilities, sign a lease, commute to school/work, run errands, balance your monthly budget.

80. Some roommates are great, some aren't. All are social learning experiences.

You will probably have roommates you admire and wish to keep as friends for decades to come. If you do, take note of what personality traits make your relationship work. You will want to look for these traits in future roommates, spouses, or business partners.

You will definitely have some roommates you despise. Learn how to let go of your anger, accept people for who they are (you don't have to like them, but you can't change them), negotiate, and compromise. You WILL need to use these skills in the future.

Safety

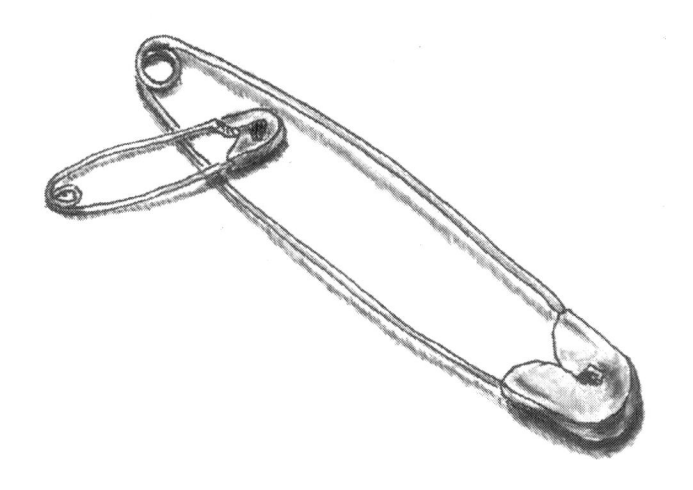

81. Consider the "Well, duh" factor.

If you leave your bike unlocked on campus, and it gets stolen, someone will probably say "Well, duh."

The "Well, duh" factor is poor decision-making that results in a predictably bad outcome. Take it into consideration when you make decisions. Wear your seatbelt, lock your door, avoid dark alleyways, etc. Start thinking ahead about the consequences of your actions, for yourself and everyone else.

NOTE: Most crime reports on my campus involve unlocked doors and walking alone at late hours. Seriously, lock your door! And read the next tip.

82. Nothing good happens after midnight.
(ok that's a bit generalized, but bear with me)

Think about it – what happens <u>before</u> midnight? Disc golf outings with friends, concerts, movies, day trips, etc. Fun and little to regret.

After midnight, the cover of darkness, tiredness, and intoxication often combine to produce very poor decisions.

Ok, so midnight is not a magical time. You can get into trouble before midnight and you can have amazing experiences (that you don't regret) after midnight. Just think a little more carefully about your decision-making process after the clock strikes twelve.

Oh! And YOU may be ok at making decisions after midnight, but other people might not be.* Avoid them! Get home. And travel with a buddy (or ten).

Most crimes occur between midnight and 1 a.m. (fbi.gov)

Money
Money
Money

83. Take loans if you have to.

On average, college provides an excellent return on your investment. Don't be afraid to take a loan. BUT, be aware of your major's rate of return. Going into engineering? You'll probably have an easier time paying those loans back. There are jobs available and they tend to have higher starting salaries. Majoring in psychology or English? You'll need to watch every penny. Take minimal loans.

If you're working a job for more than 20 hours per week, you either need loans OR you need to become a part-time student. Remember, a full-time student SHOULD be spending about 45 hours per week on school. You can't have a full-time job and get your money's worth out of college (and stay healthy).

84. Track your spending*.

Sometimes we don't realize how much we spend until we keep records. Spend one week tracking every penny – then multiply by 52 weeks. If you buy a $3 cup of coffee every day before class, that's $780 annually. Is it worth it?

Money is one of the four main reasons why people drop out of college. Do not waste a penny.

*See **Appendix F** *for a spending chart.*

85. Credit cards... and a free T-shirt!!

Let's say you either earn or have budgeted $1,000 per month. Most goes to your rent, car payment, insurance, utilities and services. When these are paid, you have $100 left over. All your remaining expenses go on a credit card with a $2,500 spending limit. How much money can you put on your credit card each month?

If you said anything more than $100, you're in trouble.

College campuses are crawling with credit card vendors, especially at the start of fall semester. They'll offer you free T-shirts, cups, Frisbees, discount coupons and more just to apply. Unfortunately, most students don't read the fine print (that awesome interest rate of 5% increases to 18% after six months or late charges start at $80). They know you better than you know them, and they're in business to make money.

Now, credit cards can be great in a lot of ways; build up your credit score or have money for emergencies, and, if the card gets stolen, you're usually not responsible for fraudulent charges). But, you absolutely MUST pay off your credit card each month. Not doing so is a MASSIVE waste. If you pay $50 in interest charges each month, that's $600 per year for nothing.

So get a credit card, but only one. And don't move your money from one credit card to another for the promise of a T-shirt or short-time benefit. Your credit score will be really important in just a few years.

86. Think long-term about money*.

When making money decisions, think about future or total expenses. For example, should you pay for a tutor at $20 an hour? At 2 hours per week and 15 weeks per semester, that's $600. Sounds like a lot! Until you consider that taking the class over when you fail is over $1,000.

Should you buy cheap plastic furniture or real furniture? Let's say cheap plastic furniture costs only $200, but it breaks or you get rid of it. You buy new items every year. In five years, you will have spent $1,000 and you still need real furniture. If you buy a couple nice, simple pieces of real furniture (used), you may spend $1,000, but you'll have them for five years and beyond. At the end of the five years, you can sell the furniture and recoup some of that $1,000. Plus, you don't contribute to the landfill.

Don't forget about upkeep costs. If you buy a vacuum for $100 that requires $50 of bags or filters per year, you'll spend $350 over 5 years. If you buy a $300 vacuum that doesn't require bags or filters, you'll spend less over the long-term.

So check the price of ink before buying a printer, the price of coffee supplies when buying a coffeemaker, and the price of updates and accessories before buying technology.

*NOTE: *Environmentally-friendly living is economically-friendly living. See* **Appendix G** *for suggestions on saving the Earth and your wallet.*

87. Slowly take over bills.

I don't think my mom and I planned it, but we ended up slowly shifting responsibility for bills over my four years at college. When I graduated, I wasn't hit with the "sticker shock" of monthly expenses like some of my friends.

Consider this arrangement:

> Freshman Year – you pay for non-essentials, extras
> Sophomore Year – add in textbook costs
> Junior Year – add in groceries/meals and utilities
> Senior Year – add in rent
> After graduating – add in insurance, car payment

You can work ~15 weeks per year full-time (summers and breaks) and ~30 weeks per year part-time (10 hours per week during school). If you net just $7 per hour after taxes, you'll earn over $4,000 per year. Not a lot. But it's enough to cover these expenses through Junior year. By that time, you should have three years of experience and can ask for a raise or promotion.

88. Reduce technology & service fees.

Between cell phones, TV/cable, computers and Internet services, you can easily spend over $100 per month JUST on service fees. Add in new devices every couple years and that number skyrockets. You can use an old cell phone, with pay-as-you-go service (no special features) for less than $20 per month. You don't need TV. You can use an older computer with public Internet services at school.

It's like driving an older car; it may not be pretty or have the latest upgrades, but if it runs reliably and is paid off, it's worth a lot of peace-of-mind. Don't be swayed by peer pressure to live outside your means.

89. Live cheap.

I once lived on $100 per month ($75 shared rent and utilities, $25 for food). This was REALLY cheap even then ($160 in today's dollars). All I owned, I could pack in my car. I didn't have a phone; I used a pay phone a couple of blocks away. I walked or rode my bike everywhere. It wasn't comfortable or healthy (pb&j and apples for every meal). BUT there is tremendous power in knowing I've done it. I know that, if things get really bad for me in the future, I've survived, temporarily, living off very little money. It's something I can overcome if necessary.

I also learned a lot about other people who lived in similar situations. The experience allowed me to see a world I would have never believed existed. It allowed me to understand that health, education, family, political representation, social structure, and environmental issues have tremendous influences on success. And it makes me appreciative of how lucky I am.

Your parents won't be happy if you live cheaply (they're used to a much higher standard of living), but you'll be happy if you aren't in debt up to your eyeballs. As long as you're safe, it's ok.

Appendices

APPENDIX A
Calendar Samples

I recommend starting with a weekly/hourly calendar (next page) on paper. Electronic calendars have useful alarms notifying you when an appointment is coming up, but they're not great for looking ahead. Paper calendars sit out on your desk, reminding you of upcoming events constantly.

Over time, I've switched to three calendars (yes, three). My weekly/hourly calendar comes with me and serves as my main calendar. I have a monthly calendar for major events (tests, start/end dates of the semester, drop deadlines, field trips, school holidays, etc.). This stays at my desk, hanging just to the side of my computer screen, reminding me of important, upcoming occasions.

My final calendar is daily. For each day of the week, I have certain tasks. For example, every Monday I teach two courses and have work associated with those (posting assignments and notes, preparing handouts, etc.), organize a weekly seminar, hold office hours, back-up my computer, and write. At the start of each semester, I compile these daily lists and print them out. Then, I tape a sheet of acetate on top and keep this daily calendar inside my weekly calendar. Each day, I cross off tasks with a Sharpie marker (the marker can also write in extra tasks). At the end of the week, I clean the acetate by wiping down with rubbing alcohol.

89 ESSENTIAL TIPS for NEW COLLEGE STUDENTS

MONTH

Monday	Tuesday 28	Wednesday 29	Thursday 30	Friday 31	Saturday 1	Sunday 2

(Weekly planner with half-hour time slots from 6:00 AM to 9:00 PM for each day, with NOTES sections.)

APPENDIX B
Note-Taking Hints

Get used to making a mess of your notes. Organize and rewrite them after class.

Place the date and topic of the lecture at the top of the page. The beginning of the lecture will often contain a list of topics to be covered that day (e.g., "Today we'll cover the diversity of reptiles and amphibians. We'll examine the characteristics of each group, classification of subgroups, and evolutionary emergences and declines."). The remainder of the class will go into detail on each of these subjects. If you remember the major topics, details will be less overwhelming.

When you take notes, you'll probably include many, many details. Most students think it's their job to memorize all of them individually (e.g., the definition of carapace or urostyle, specific dates, scientific names, and how much oxygen can cross semi-permeable skin).

Any professor will tell you that the main focus should be on making connections and being able to relate information.

In your notes, try to outline the information. Group related information together (draw a circle or box around it). If your professor makes a connection between two concepts, circle them both and connect with a line.

Your professor isn't just wasting breath up there. If s/he is repeating an idea, it's an important concept. Underline it.

Your notes should be a mess when you leave class. Schedule time later to re-write, re-organize, and review the material. This step ensures you understand the material (you can't organize it if you don't understand it). If something doesn't make sense, check your textbook or e-resources or email your professor for clarification.

When you've finished neatening and organizing your notes (probably 2–5 pages), make a half-sheet outline from the major points of the lecture. Concentrate on this for most of your studying.

Lastly, don't be afraid to draw – timelines, graphs, anatomy, maps, etc. You can even draw organizational charts rather than outlining your notes. For our example lecture covering reptile and amphibian diversity, a summarizing organizational chart may look like this:

NOTE: Learn to abbreviate. An underlined "n" in superscript is the abbreviation for "-tion." So "pop$\underline{n}$" is "population."

Reptile & Amphib. Diversity

	Characteristics	Subgroups	Evol.

Amphibians	Larva in H₂O - eat algae
	Permeable skin (exchange gasses)
	3-chamber heart
		Lissamphibia
		- Anura (frog/toad)
		- Caudata (salam.)
		  Hellbender = prim.
		  Salam. = intern. fert.
		  Siren = aqt-live
		- Apoda (caecilian)
			From pop'n of Sarcopterygian fish (Devonian ~400mya)
			↑ in Carboniferous
			*current decline in pop'ns / extinct

	Both: Ectothermic Adults carnivores Amniote eggs		
Reptiles	Eggs w/ shells ↳ some live births Scales (↓ H₂O loss) 3.5-chambered heart ↳ ventricle	Squamata (lizards + snakes) Testudines (turtles) Sphenodontia (tuatara) Crocodilia ↳ *closest relative to birds	From pop'n of amphib.s (Carboniferous ~300 mya) Major extinct. 65 mya • mammals & birds evolved from reptilian pop'ns

APPENDIX C
Organization and Retrieval Practice

Once you've made your half-page outline or organization chart, use it to study. Time yourself for three minutes. Review the Reptile/Amphibian Diversity lecture chart and try to recreate it on the following page.

NOTE: As you complete this activity, you'll catch on to some sections quickly and struggle with others. Use mnemonics to help you through the trouble spots. For instance, if you're having a difficult time remembering the Reptile and Amphibian subgroups, try creating a goofy sentence using the first letter of each word, like "Large Ants Cause Apple Sauce To Smell Crummy." Sometimes, just remembering the number of items in each location can help too.

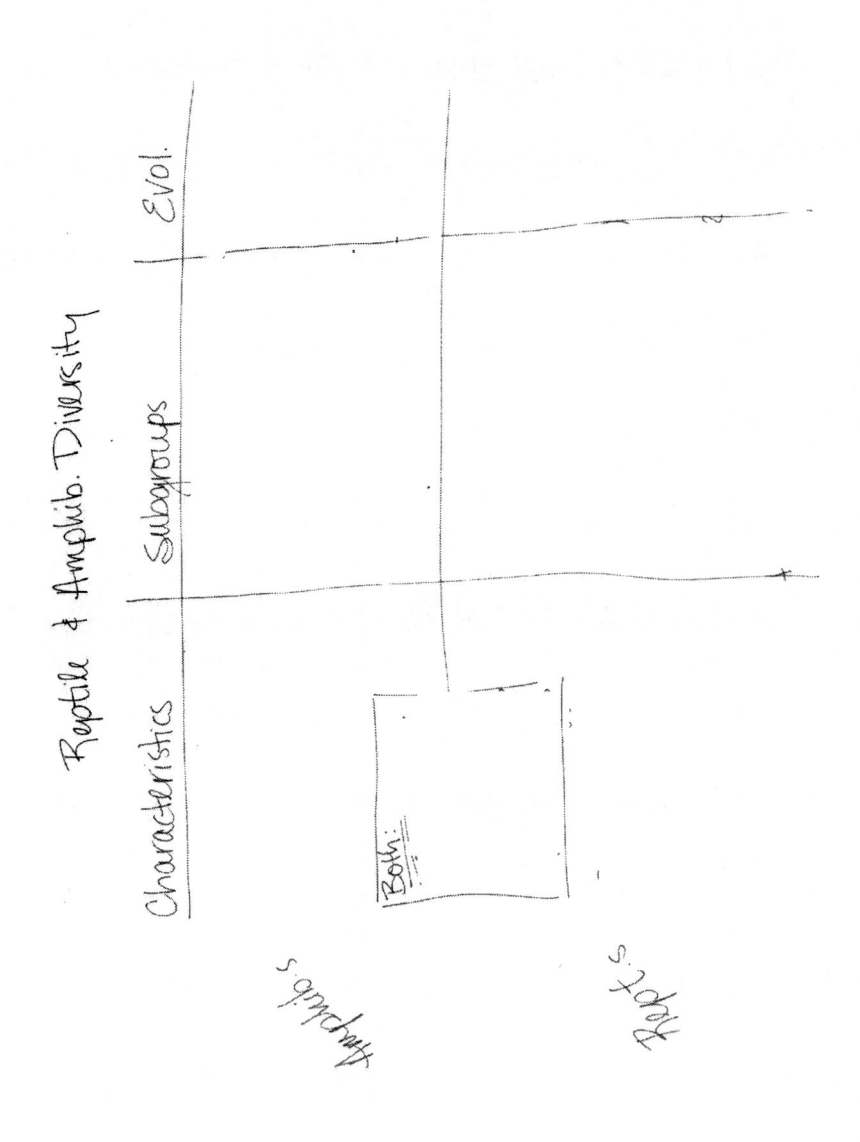

Reptile & Amphib. Diversity

Characteristics	Subgroups	Evol.
Both:		

Amphibs
Rept's

When your three minutes is up, count how many correct lines you wrote in the correct places. Divide by 31 (the total number of concepts in the chart). That's your grade.

Give yourself another three minutes and try again. Keep trying until you get 90–100%.

Organize your notes and do this *Retrieval* activity after each lecture. Then, over the weekend, repeat your *Retrieval* activities for all the week's lectures. Before each test, do your *Retrieval* activities for all the lectures covered AND re-read your notes to pick up any remaining details.

This works because you're grouping information into clumps which has two benefits. First, clumping information means you have to find similar items and relate one to another. By grouping and subgrouping facts, you recognize themes in the subject. Second, we remember clumped information better (a telephone number is easier to remember as 214-868-6309 than as 2148686309). Try to keep your "clumps" to three to five items.

APPENDIX D
Editing Examples

Let's look at the following paragraph to see how we can improve it:

The Civil War was a very important turning point in American history. Many factors contributed to the start and longevity of the war, including slavery, economic and social systems. When comparing daguerreotypes from the antebellum to reconstruction eras, a clear picture of onerous autonomy, disenfranchisement of scalawags, and annihilated infrastructure emerges. Perhaps the war may not have improved the South in some situations.

Make every sentence valuable: The first sentence doesn't explain anything. Why was the Civil War important? How did it impact American history? How did society shift from before the war to after? Never say something is "important" or "interesting." Rather, explain why.

The Civil War shifted the agrarian American South from system of slavery to one reliant on sharecroppers.

Don't make your reader work to figure out what you're saying: Is the second sentence suggesting that the three systems led to the start of the war? Or the longevity? Or both?

While the war started mostly over slavery issues, the aggression progressed as more Southerners felt their economic and social systems attacked.

Don't show off specific terminology when you don't understand the big picture: Do you feel like you need a dictionary to grasp the third sentence? Limit technical terms and write as though you're communicating professionally with a peer. If your friends don't understand these words, avoid them.

Photographs document the economic and social strains that emerged after the War.

If you have to write too many qualifiers, your statement isn't a strong one: The last sentence is as wishy-washy as you can get – "perhaps," "may not," and "some." Limit qualifiers to one per sentence.

While the war resulted in an improved life for many people, the infrastructure and economic strains continued for decades.

APPENDIX E
Total Health Checklist

Your health is between you and your doctor. Sometimes, though, we think of "health" as just illnesses or physical fitness. This basic checklist is a daily starting point for your to consider your sleep patterns, eating habits, and mental status. If we take a few moments to really consider "how do I feel?", we can make small adjustments before things get out of hand.

Sleep:

> Hours of sleep? ____ (aim for 8–9 hours)
> Quality of sleep – Excellent... OK... Poor

Remember to take your **medications**?

Exercise: (aim for 30–60 minutes/day; alternate categories)
> Stretching/Flexibility training
> Cardiovascular training
> Weights/Resistance training

Meditation/Reflection

Be thankful and aware of the positives in your life, place the negatives in perspective, and just take a few moments to breathe deeply and sense your mental state.

Meals:

> Water at each meal (limit sugary beverages)
> Fruit, Vegetable & Protein at each meal (proteins include more than just meat; try peanut butter, cheese, beans, nuts, or eggs)

Limit TV/Computer time (besides school/work assignments)

Get outside! Sunshine and fresh air do a world of good.

APPENDIX F

Spending Chart

This list is divided into three sections. The first section consists of general necessities (housing, utilities, food, insurance). Cars are not necessary, but often expected when looking for work. A car may allow you to live in a less expensive location. If you can do without one though, great! The point of Section 1 is to estimate your bare-minimum expenses. You must have enough saved up or be able to earn enough to cover these monthly bills. If you don't, you'll need to figure out ways to cut these expenses (get a roommate, find a cheaper phone plan, etc.) or make more money.

The second section contains your next priorities if you plan to stay in college. Even if you only put $10 into savings per month, make sure to do that before spending any money for items in Section 3.

If you're taking out student loans, use that money ONLY to cover Section 1 or 2 expenses.

The third section includes extraneous items. Some people think "clothes" should be in Section 1, but clothes don't need to be replaced yearly like they did when you were younger. You're not growing much anymore. Also, most college students don't need fancy clothing. If you need new clothes, buy classic styles and quality fabrics so you can keep them for years to come.

89 ESSENTIAL TIPS for NEW COLLEGE STUDENTS

Section 1:

- Rent & Renter's Insurance
- Utilities (electricity/gas, water, waste, internet, phone)
- Health Insurance
- Doctor/Dentist Visits & Prescriptions
- Car Payment & Repairs, Car Insurance/Taxes, Gas
- Food (for cooking, not eating out – See Section 3)
- Home Basics (soap, toilet paper, cookware, blankets, etc.)

Section 2:

- Tuition & Books
- Savings

Section 3:

- Hobbies
- Entertainment/Eating Out
- Gifts & Shipping
- Donations
- Clothes & Accessories, Makeup, etc.
- Home Décor/Extras
- Travel
- Miscellaneous/Unexpected Expenses

Use the spending chart (next page) to track your monthly expenses. When you make a monthly payment, record it in the appropriate white box. Place the date of your payment in the grey box underneath. When the expense is pulled from your account, highlight the entry so you know it has cleared.

When you receive a credit card statement, review the charges and classify each as a Section 1, 2, or 3 expense. Those three "Credit Card" categories should equal the amount on your bill.

It's a good idea to keep a piece of paper tracking all your expenses. Each time you spend money, get a receipt. At the end of the day, write all those figures down (and categorize them as Section 1, 2, or 3). Highlight any items you paid with your credit card so you'll know what to expect on your next bill. Add the cash-payment sums to your spending chart.

At the end of each month, add up your monthly payments to see your total expenses. See if you can spend less the next month. At the end of the year, total each billing category. Is there anything you can cut back on for next year?

Keep this chart as a record so you'll know what to expect next year.

89 ESSENTIAL TIPS for NEW COLLEGE STUDENTS

BILL	Jan.	Feb.	Mar.	Apr.	May	June	July	Aug.	Sept.	Oct.	Nov.	Dec.
Rent (+insur.) or Mortgage												
Electricity / Gas												
Water / Waste												
Internet / Phone												
Car payment (+insur.)												
Health Insurance												
Savings												
Credit Card (Section 1)												
Credit Card (Section 2)												
Credit Card (Section 3)												
Misc.:												
TOTAL												

A few words about insurance and savings:

Yes, insurance is necessary. If you can't afford basic monthly insurance payments, you certainly will not be able to afford the consequences of being uninsured.

As for your savings account, here's a chart with savings goals:

Age	Savings Goal
25	0.5 x annual income
30	1 x annual income
35	2 x annual income
40	4 x annual income
50	7 x annual income
60	10 x annual income

If you do some of the math, you'll see why "Savings" is in Section 2. Get used to saving a chunk of your income now, and life will be much easier for years to come.

APPENDIX G
Eco-Friendly Living (Economics & Ecosystems)

Smart ecological decisions are the same as smart long-term economic (and health) decisions. It's better to buy a quality product once than a cheap product many times; it's better to spend a little more on quality food and require fewer health care visits in the future.

Live well. Think long-term. Choose wisely.

Energy

- Keep thermostats on 68°F in the winter and 78°F in the summer.
- Plug devices into surge protectors. Turn off the surge protectors when you leave the house or go to bed. Many devices, like TVs and music players, use energy even when turned off.
- Walk or bike when possible (and safe).
- Minimize trips – consolidate errands or stop on the way from work or school.
- When you consider buying or renting a house, remember that larger houses require more heat, A/C, furniture, lighting… everything, in the long-term.
- Take the stairs (not the elevator); open the door yourself (don't use the handicap button) – unless you really need these devices, of course!
- Use a manual can opener (not electric), a push-mower (not riding), a rake (not leaf blower), etc.

Water

- Use less water. When purchasing appliances, check their water usage.
- Install low-flow faucets and shower heads. Often, you won't even notice the difference, except in your water bill.
- Install a showerhead turn-off button. If you replace your shower head, consider installing a button to turn off the water flow. You can turn off the water at the showerhead while you lather up, then easily turn it back on (at the right temperature) to rinse off.
- Use a low-flow toilet or add a brick in the tank.
- Use what only what you need. (Pay attention to running a faucet without actually using the water, like running water while you brush your teeth.)

Buying Stuff

- Buy events for loved ones, not things (especially things they don't really need).
- Refill, instead of buying new (like hand soap – refill containers use less packaging than buying new pumps). Use a refillable water bottle!!!
- Don't buy it unless you need it. (How many pairs of shoes do you actually NEED?)
- Replace items when they're BROKEN.
- Really want something new? Consider delaying the purchase (e.g., buying a new phone every 3 years, not every 2 years, means ~12 fewer phones over your life). This also reduces impulse purchases.

- Buy quality items that can be cleaned and reused; don't buy disposables.
- Buy local when possible. You'll support your local economy AND save energy spent on shipping.
- Use rags to clean, not paper towels. Old T-shirts and socks make great rags.

Make Your Own

- Grow a garden even if it's just one tomato or basil plant.
- Make paper decorations. Don't buy plastic decorations from far-away countries.
- Make your own cleaning products: vinegar, baking soda, and ammonia clean just about anything (look online for "recipes.")
- Learn to cook – STOP EATING PROCESSED FOODS. Read the ingredients. If the list has words you don't recognize, you probably shouldn't be eating it.
- Eat more plants, less meat. You don't have to become a vegetarian, just try a meat-less day or meal.

Feeling overwhelmed? Just try one tip at a time.

What's Your 90th Tip?

ABOUT THE AUTHOR

J.M. Landin began her scholarly career as a less-than-stellar student. She stumbled her way through eleven years of undergraduate and graduate programs. During that time, she accidentally made some very smart decisions in addition to a LOT of mistakes described in this book.

After graduating with her bachelor of science in biology, J.M. Landin worked as an artist, pharmacy technician, wildlife trapper, website developer, medical researcher, etc. In time, she made a major career decision (described in this book [Tip #76]) and returned to school for a master's degree in biology and PhD in Science Education.

Today, Dr. Landin is a professor and advisor at a large research university in North Carolina. She teaches and advises hundreds of students each semester.

Made in the USA
Lexington, KY
03 May 2017